THE OFFICE HUMOUR B·O·O·K

Pete Fagan and Mark Schaffer

Illustrations by Drew Pallo

ANGUS & ROBERTSON PUBLISHERS

ANGUS & ROBERTSON PUBLISHERS

Unit 4, Eden Park, 31 Waterloo Road,
North Ryde, NSW, Australia 2113, and
16 Golden Square, London W1R 4BN,
United Kingdom

First published in the USA by
Harmony Books in 1985
First published in the United Kingdom by
Angus & Robertson (UK) Ltd in 1986

Published by arrangement with Harmony Books,
a Division of Crown Publishers, Inc.

Copyright © 1985 by
Pete Fagan and Mark Schaffer

ISBN 0 207 15312 4

Printed in the United Kingdom

This book is respectfully dedicated to the father of xerography, CHESTER F. CARLSON, who, alas, never realized the entertainment potential of his invention, the photocopier.

Introduction

The photocopier has often been credited with "revolutionizing" office work, but it's never been acknowledged as the cause of a revolution in office humour. Until now. For with the dawn of the copier came a proliferation of cartoons, jokes, spoofs, fables, and satires about life at the office. Hardly a day has passed since the first machine was plugged in, that some company comic hasn't sneaked up to it to run off ten copies of the latest piece of underground humour.

Workers have always poked fun at the boss, the workplace, their jobs, the system, and themselves. Anonymously, Swivel-Chair Philosophers and Coffee-Break Cartoonists have verbally and pictorially folded, spindled, and mutilated every aspect of the 9 to 5 haul. Who are these mysterious wise guys and girls? No one knows. They're folk humorists in three-piece suits. Sit-down comics in silk blouses and designer jeans. Corporate hecklers in overalls.

No business or industry is safe. Anonymous office humour has shown up in High-Tech puzzle palaces, farm machinery factories, teachers' staffrooms, church vestries, TV newsrooms and salesmen's sample cases. No underground network of radical pamphleteers could hold a candle to the distribution network of these silly subversives. Some of our examples have been found as close as the corner petrol station and as far away as a prestigious bank in Brisbane, Australia.

Here, for the first time, is a collection of the best in anonymous office humour. If you've ever worked in an office, if you've ever had a boss, if your career, financial future, and mental health have ever been in the hands of "upper management", you're going to feel at home in these pages.

Acknowledgments

A "thank you" to the following friends and acquaintances who provided some of the examples of office humour used in the collection: Bob Abel, Diane Bridge, Lois Cohen, Ray Dumont, Claudia Ellis, Nancy Franus, Ruth Ghormley, Renee Jackson, Burt Levine, Barbara Martin, Dan McGarrigan, Gary Mrenak, Rev. Roy Riley, B.J. Silvey, Jan and Cary Smolen, and Tom Spellerberg.

Many thanks to Carole Geisler and Bill Wagner for their assistance in the development of this book and special appreciation to Chris Mueller for all her efforts during the book's production and for her valuable contribution to our campaign to place our project before a sympathetic publisher. Special thanks also to Drew Pallo, our artist, who took crumpled, blotchy, faded photocopies from our business-humour collection and, with the right touch of original artwork here and there, produced some terrific pieces of office humour. And thanks to Lou Damis, who gave Pete Fagan his first taste of office folklore eighteen years ago and started all this.

NOBODY OF THE YEAR

AWARD

This Is To Certify That

_____

has been selected by the AWARDS COMMITTEE
as the man most qualified for this distinguished award.
His accomplishments, activities, and expended energy
have been completely negligible and absurd.
In grateful recognition of a most useless individual
the BOARD OF GOVERNORS hereby presents this award

X_____

X_____

Date:_____

THE ALL-PURPOSE BUSINESSMAN'S VOCABULARY

A CONSULTANT - Any ordinary guy with a briefcase more than 50 miles from home.

AN EXPERT - A person who avoids all small errors as he sweeps toward the grand fallacy.

A STATISTICIAN - One who draws a mathematically precise line from an unwarranted assumption to a foregone conclusion.

A COLLEAGUE - Someone called in at the last minute to share the blame.

A RELIABLE SOURCE - The guy you just met.

AN INFORMED SOURCE - The guy who told the guy you just met.

AN UNIMPEACHABLE SOURCE - The guy who started the rumor originally.

A MEETING - A mass mulling of master-minds.

A CONFERENCE - A place where conversation is substituted for the dreariness of labor and the loneliness of thought.

A PROGRAM - Any assignment that can't be completed by one telephone call.

CHANNELS - The guy who has a desk between two expeditors.

TO ACTIVATE - To make copies and add more names to the memo.

TO EXPEDITE - To confound confusion with commotion.

TO IMPLEMENT A PROGRAM - Hire more people and expand the office.

TO RESEARCH - Go looking for the jerk who moved the files.

TO GIVE SOMEONE THE PICTURE - To present a long, confused and inaccurate statement to a newcomer.

TO CLARIFY - To fill in the background with so many details that the foreground goes underground.

LONELY?

Like To Meet New People?
Like A Change?
Like Excitement?
Like A New Job?

Just Make One
More Cock-Up!

RUSH JOB CALENDAR

NEG	FRI	FRI	THU	WED	TUE	MON
8	7	6	5	4	3	2
16	15	14	13	12	11	9
23	22	21	20	19	18	17
31	30	29	28	27	26	24
38	37	36	35	34	33	32

1. EVERY JOB IS IN A RUSH. EVERYONE WANTS HIS JOB YESTERDAY. WITH THIS CALENDAR, A CUSTOMER CAN ORDER HIS WORK ON THE 7th, AND HAVE IT DELIVERED ON THE 3rd.

2. ALL CUSTOMERS WANT THEIR JOBS ON FRIDAY. . .SO THERE ARE TWO FRIDAYS IN EACH WEEK.

3. THERE ARE SEVEN EXTRA DAYS AT THE END-OF-THE-MONTH FOR THOSE END-OF-THE-MONTH JOBS.

4. THERE WILL BE NO FIRST OF THE MONTH BILLS TO BE PAID, AS THERE ISN'T ANY "FIRST." THE "TENTH" AND "TWENTY-FIFTH" ALSO HAVE BEEN OMITTED—IN CASE YOU HAVE BEEN ASKED TO PAY ON ONE OF THESE DAYS.

5. THERE ARE NO BOTHERSOME NON-PRODUCTIVE SATURDAYS AND SUNDAYS. NO TIME AND ONE HALF OR DOUBLE TIME TO PAY.

6. THERE'S A NEW DAY EACH WEEK CALLED—NEGOTIATION DAY.

Executive Pass the
BUCK SLIP

DATE

TO

READ &

☐ Return
☐ Retain
☐ Route

ACTION

☐ Review & Summarize
☐ Review & Recommend
☐ Take Note
☐ Report Highlights
☐ Translate Into English
☐ Lose in Round File
☐ Read & Weep
☐ Read & Destroy
☐ Destroy While Reading
☐ Destroy Before Reading
☐ Read & Pass On
☐ Read & Pass Out
☐ Prepare Letter
☐ Answer Letter
☐ Follow Up & Report
☐ For Your Eyes Only
☐ Let's Discuss
☐ It's Up To You
☐ None Of The Above

PERFORMANCE RATINGS

PERFORMANCE FACTORS	EXCELLENT Far Exceeds Job Requirements	VERY GOOD Exceeds Job Requirements	GOOD Meets Job Requirements	FAIR Needs Some Improvement	UNSATISFACTORY Does Not Meet Minimum Req't
QUALITY	Leaps tall buildings with a single bound	Must take running start to leap over tall buildings	Can only leap over a short building, or medium with no spikes	Crashes into buildings when attempting to jump over them	Cannot recognize building at all, let alone jump it
TIMELINESS	Is faster than a speeding bullet	Is as fast as a speeding bullet	Not quite as fast as a speeding bullet	Would you believe a slow bullet?	Wounds self with bullets when attempting to shoot gun
INITIATIVE	Is stronger than a locomotive	Is stronger than a bull elephant	Is stronger than a bull	Shoots the bull	Smells like a bull
ADAPTABILITY	Walks on water consistently	Walks on water in emergencies	Walks with water	Drinks water	Passes water in emergencies
COMMUNICATION	Talks with God	Talks with the Angels	Talks to himself	Argues with himself	Loses arguments with himself

The Six Phases Of A Project

1. ENTHUSIASM

2. DISILLUSIONMENT

3. PANIC

4. SEARCH FOR THE GUILTY

5. PUNISHMENT OF THE INNOCENT

6. PRAISE & HONORS FOR THE NONPARTICIPANTS

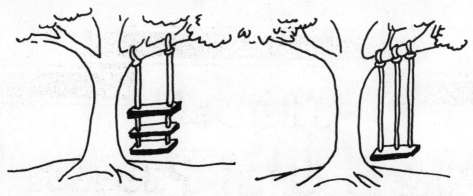

**As proposed by
the project sponsor.**

**As specified in
the project request.**

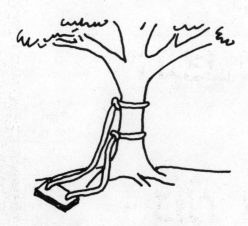

**As designed by
the senior analyst.**

**As produced by
the programmers.**

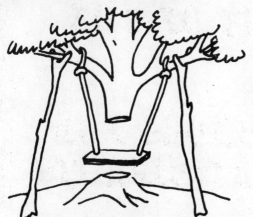

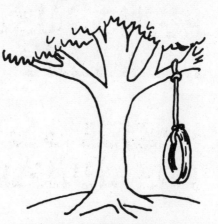

**As installed at
the user's site.**

**What the user
wanted.**

STATE OF THE ART
BUZZ WORD
PHRASEOLOGY

Anyone who is familiar with the academic, business or government worlds knows that there seems to be a rule that says "When choosing between a simple and a more abstract term, always pick the more confusing one."

In the past, this has been a great setback for clear-headed writers and speakers. But now modern technology has found a solution: the Systematic Buzz Phrase Synthesizer.

The synthesizer is simple to use. Whenever you want to say nothing in an authoritative way, simply pick any three-digit number, and then find the matching word from each column. For example, 424 produces "functional monitored programming," which should impress anyone untrained in detecting high-level abstractions.

	COLUMN 1		COLUMN 2		COLUMN 3
0	Integrated	0	Management	0	Options
1	Total	1	Organizational	1	Flexibility
2	Systematized	2	Monitored	2	Capability
3	Parallel	3	Reciprocal	3	Mobility
4	Functional	4	Digital	4	Programming
5	Responsive	5	Logistical	5	Concept
6	Optional	6	Transitional	6	Time-phase
7	Synchronized	7	Incremental	7	Projection
8	Compatible	8	Third-generation	8	Hardware
9	Balanced	9	Policy	9	Contingency

WHAT WE HAVE HERE
IS A FAILURE TO COMMUNICATE!
OR

(WHAT THAT FAMILIAR PHRASE REALLY MEANS)

"IT IS IN PROCESS" - So wrapped in red tape that the situation is almost hopeless.

"WE WILL LOOK INTO IT" - By the time the wheel makes a full turn, we assume you will have forgotten about it.

"WILL ADVISE YOU IN DUE COURSE" - If we figure it out, we'll let you know.

"WE ARE AWARE OF IT" - We had hoped that the fool who started it would have forgotten about it by this time.

"IT'S UNDER CONSIDERATION" - Never heard of it.

"UNDER ACTIVE CONSIDERATION" - We are looking in the files for it.

"WE ARE MAKING A SURVEY" - We need more time to think of an answer.

"LET'S GET TOGETHER ON THIS" - I'm assuming you're as confused as I am.

"PLEASE NOTE AND INITIAL" - Let's spread the responsibility for this.

"GIVE US THE BENEFIT OF YOUR PRESENT THINKING" - We'll listen to what you have to say as long as it doesn't interfere with what we have already decided to do.

"GIVE US YOUR INTERPRETATION" - Your warped opinion will be pitted against your adversary's good sense.

"SEE ME" or "LET'S DISCUSS" - Come down to my office, I'm lonesome.

THIRTEEN RULES FOR THE WITLESS
OR
HOW TO SUCCEED WITHOUT TALENT

1. Study to look tremendously important.

2. Speak with great assurance. Stick to generally accepted facts, however.

3. Avoid arguments; if challenged, fire an irrelevant question at your antagonist and intently polish your glasses while he tries to answer. As an alternative, hum under your breath while examining your fingernails.

4. Contrive to mingle with important people.

5. Before talking with a man you wish to impress, ferret out his remedies for current problems, then advocate them strongly.

6. Listen while others wrangle. Pluck out a platitude and defend it righteously.

7. When asked a question by a subordinate, give him a "have you lost your mind" stare until he glances down, then paraphrase the question back at him.

8. Acquire a capable stooge, but keep him in the background.

9. In offering to perform a service, imply your complete familiarity.

10. Arrange to be the clearinghouse for all complaints - it encourages the thought that you are in control.

11. Never acknowledge thanks for your attention; this will implant subconscious obligation in the mind of your victim.

12. Carry yourself in the grand manner. Refer to your associates as "some of the boys in our office." Discourage light conversation that might bridge the gap between boss and man.

13. Walk swiftly from place to place as if engrossed in affairs of great moment. Keep your office door closed. Interview by appointment only and give orders by memoranda. Remember, you are a big shot and you don't give a damn who knows it.

NOTICE!

The objective of all dedicated managers should be to thoroughly analyze all situations, anticipate all problems prior to their occurrence, have answers for these problems and move swiftly to solve these problems when called upon . . . .

However

When You Are Up To Your Arse In Alligators, It Is Difficult To Remind Yourself That Your Initial Objective Was To Drain The Swamp!

NO UNAUTHORIZED DISCLOSURES

Protect Classified Information

WE HAVE READ YOUR PROPOSAL...

...AND ARE GIVING IT

SERIOUS CONSIDERATION.

TO ALL EMPLOYEES

Due to increased competition and a keen desire to remain
in business, we find it necessary to institute a new policy—

EFFECTIVE IMMEDIATELY

We are asking that somewhere between starting and
quitting time and without infringing too much on the time
usually devoted to lunch period, coffee breaks, rest periods,
story telling, ticket selling, vacation planning, and the
rehashing of yesterday's TV programs, that each employee
endeavor to find some time that can be set aside and known
as the "WORK BREAK."

To some, this may seem a radical innovation, but
we honestly believe the idea has great possibilities. It
can conceivably be an aid to steady employment and it
might also be a means of assuring regular pay.

While the adoption of the Work Break Plan is
not compulsory, it is hoped that each employee will
find enough time to give the plan a fair trial.

The Management

INTERNAL MEMORANDUM

TO: ALL PERSONNEL

FROM: Al Phabet

SUBJ: Death of Company Employees

It has been brought to our attention that many employees are dying and refusing to fall over after they are dead. This must stop.

On or after 15 December, any employee found sitting up after he has died will be dropped from the payroll at once (i.e. within 90 days). Where it can be proven that the employee is being supported by a typewriter or other company property, an additional 90 days will be granted. The following procedure will be strictly followed:

If after several hours, it is noted a worker has not moved, or changed position, the supervisor will investigate. Because of the highly sensitive nature of our employees and the close resemblance between death and their natural working attitude, the investigation will be made quietly so as not to disturb the employee if he has fallen asleep. If some doubt exists as to the true condition of the employee, extending a pay cheque is a fine test. If the employee does not reach for it, it may be reasonably assumed that he is dead. In some cases the instinct is so strongly developed, however, that a spasmodic clutch or reflex action may be encountered. Don't let this fool you.

In all cases, a sworn statement by the dead person must be filled out. Fifteen (15) copies will be made, three copies are sent to the relevant government department, and three copies are retained by the deceased. Destroy the rest.

An application for permanent leave must also be filled out by the employee. Be sure to include the correct forwarding address. If he cannot write, his signature must be witnessed by two other employees, preferably alive. Complete the case by pushing the body to one side to make room for the next incumbent.

By Order of:

Dr Rigor Mortis, M.D.

Distribution: All Dead Company Employees

BEFORE YOU ASK ME FOR THE DAY OFF, CONSIDER THE FOLLOWING STATISTICS:

THERE ARE 365 DAYS IN THE YEAR, YOU SLEEP EIGHT HOURS A DAY
MAKING 122 DAYS, WHICH SUBTRACTED FROM 365 DAYS MAKES 243
DAYS. YOU ALSO HAVE 8 HOURS RECREATION EVERY DAY MAKING
ANOTHER 122 DAYS AND LEAVES A BALANCE OF 121 DAYS.
THERE ARE 52 SUNDAYS THAT YOU DO NOT WORK AT ALL,
WHICH LEAVES 69 DAYS. YOU GET SATURDAY AFTERNOON OFF,
THIS GIVES 52 HALFDAYS, OR 26 MORE DAYS THAT YOU DO NOT
WORK. THIS LEAVES A BALANCE OF 43 DAYS.
YOU GET AN HOUR OFF FOR LUNCH, WHICH WHEN TOTALED
MAKES 16 DAYS, LEAVING 27 DAYS OF THE YEAR.
YOU GET AT LEAST 21 DAYS LEAVE EVERY YEAR, SO THAT LEAVES 6 DAYS.
YOU GET 5 LEGAL HOLIDAYS DURING THE YEAR, WHICH LEAVES ONLY ONE DAY,

AND I'LL BE DAMNED IF I'LL GIVE YOU THAT ONE DAY OFF!!!!!!!!!!!!!

ATTENTION: ALL PERSONNEL

SUBJECT: EXCESSIVE ABSENCES

THE FOLLOWING RULES ARE IN EFFECT:

SICKNESS

Absolutely no excuses. We will no longer accept your doctor's statement as proof, as we believe that if you are able to go to the doctor, you are able to come to work.

LEAVE OF ABSENCE FOR AN OPERATION

We are no longer allowing this practice. We wish to discourage any thoughts that you may need an operation, as we believe that as long as you are an employee here you will need all of whatever you have, and you should not consider having anything removed. We hired you as you are and to have anything removed would certainly make you less than we bargained for.

ACCIDENTS

Our safety programs and company policy preclude any lost time for accidents. First aid in most instances will be treated during normal breaks. Application of splints, hemorrhage and artificial respiration may be done at other times, work load permitting.

DEATH (OTHER THAN YOUR OWN)

This is no excuse. There is nothing you can do for them and there is always someone else with a lesser position who can attend to the arrangements. However, if the funeral can be held in the later afternoon, we will be glad to let you off one hour early, provided your share of the work is ahead enough to keep the job going in your absence.

DEATH (YOUR OWN)

This will be accepted as an excuse, but a two week notice is required as we feel it is your duty to teach someone else your job.

RESTROOM PRIVILEGES

ENTIRELY TOO MUCH TIME IS BEING SPENT IN THE RESTROOM. In the future we will practice going in alphabetical order. For instance, those with names beginning with "A" will go from 8:00 to 8:15, "B" will go from 8:15 to 8:30, and so on. If you are unable to go at your appointed time, it will be necessary to wait until the next day when your turn comes again.

IT IS DIFFICULT TO SOAR WITH EAGLES...

WHEN YOU WORK WITH TURKEYS !

Never try to teach a pig to sing,

it wastes your time and it annoys the pig.

GETTING <u>ANYTHING</u> DONE
AROUND HERE
IS LIKE
MATING ELEPHANTS

- It's a huge undertaking

- It's accomplished with a lot of roaring and screaming

- It takes two years to get any results

NO ENEMY
WOULD DARE
BOMB THIS
PLACE AND
END THIS
CONFUSION!

*Doing a good job around
here is like wetting
your pants in a
dark suit...*

*You get a
warm feeling
but no one else
notices.*

NO JOB IS COMPLETE 'TIL
THE PAPERWORK IS DONE

The Bitterness

Of Poor Quality

Remains

Long After

The Sweetness Of

Meeting The Schedule

Has Been

Forgotten

Remember...

Sometimes The Dragon Wins

EVERYONE SHOULD BELIEVE IN SOMETHING;

I BELIEVE I'LL HAVE ANOTHER BEER.

If you can't dazzle them with brilliance, baffle them with bullshit.

YOU WANT IT WHEN?!

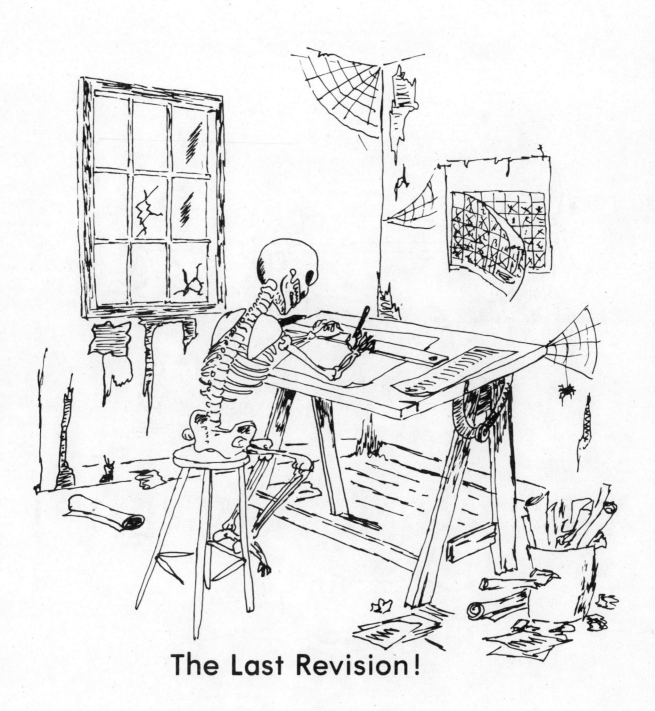

The Last Revision!

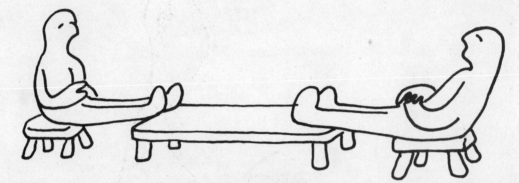

"One of these days we ought to get reorganized."

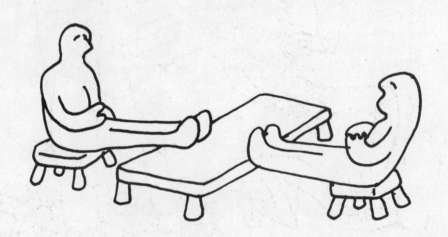

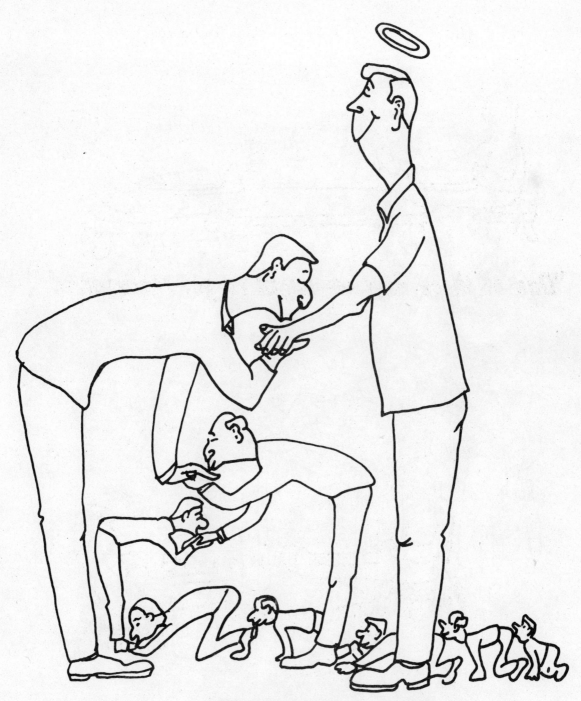

ORGANIZATIONAL CHART

"SYSTEM BEEN DOWN LONG?"

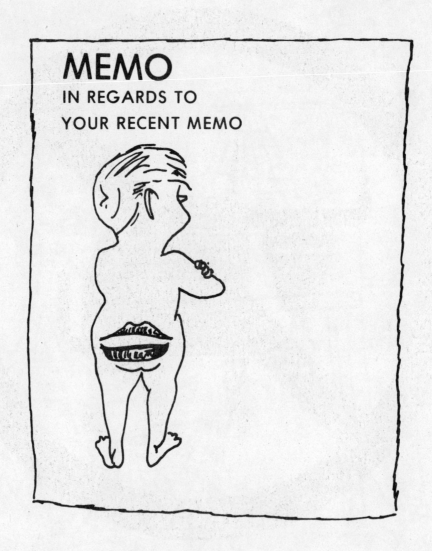

Simplified Tax Declaration Form

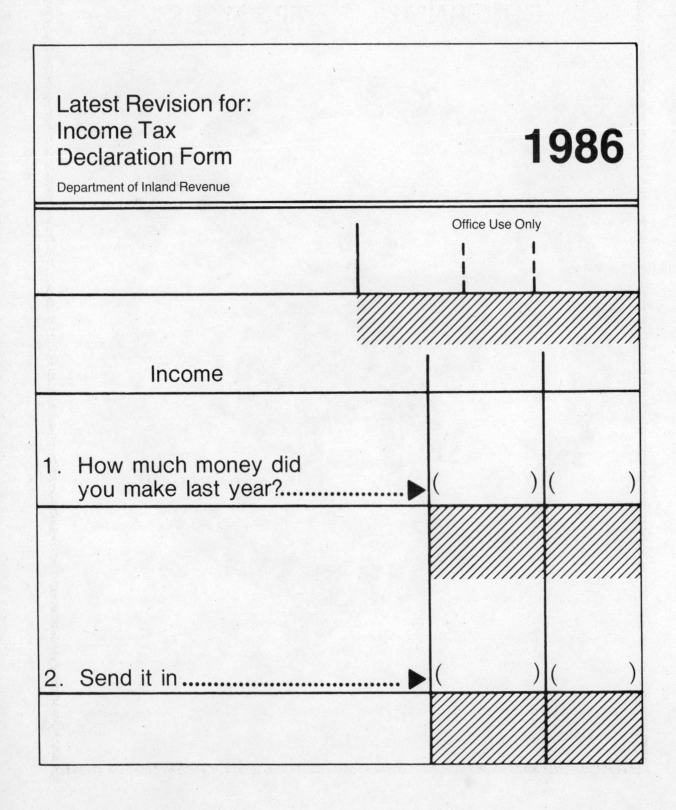

Latest Revision for:
Income Tax
Declaration Form

1986

Department of Inland Revenue

Office Use Only

Income

1. How much money did
you make last year?.................... ▶ ( ) ( )

2. Send it in .... ▶ ( ) ( )

RECOMMENDED COURSES FOR GOVERNMENT EMPLOYEES

SOCIAL SCIENCES:

      Creative Suffering
      Overcoming Peace of Mind
      Guilt Without Sex
      The Primal Shrug
      Ego Gratification Through Violence
      Dealing with Post-Self-Realization Depression
      Working Your Way Up Through Alienation

BUSINESS:

      Money and Family Inheritance Can Make You Successful
      Packaging, Marketing & Selling Your Own Body
      Underachievers Guide to Very Small Business & Consulting
         Opportunities

MENTAL HEALTH & PHYSICAL FITNESS:

      Exorcism and Acne
      Biofeedback and How to Stop
      Optional Body Functions
      Tap Dance Your Way to the Top
      Getting to Work on Time and Maintaining Regularity
      Self-Actualization Through Masochism
      The Role of Suicide in Optimal Health Maintenance
      Preservation, Repair & Maintenance of Virginity (An Introduction)

FOR WOMEN ONLY:

      Sleeping Your Way Up the Corporate Ladder
      100 Ways to Avoid Photocopying & Making Coffee
      Assertiveness: How Not to Do Windows, Floors & Typing
      Eye Contact Which Penetrates the Groin
      From Mother Earth to Dragon Lady with Dignity
      Intimidation Through Castration
      Why Every Prince Turns into a Toad

(Failure in more than one of the above makes this next course mandatory)

      How to Be a Kept Woman and Like It

```
**************************************************************************
**************************************************************************
```

YOU KNOW IT'S GOING TO BE A BAD DAY WHEN:

1. You wake up face-down on the pavement.

2. You put your bra on backwards and it fits better.

3. You call Suicide Prevention and they put you on HOLD.

4. You see the "That's Life" team waiting for you in your office.

5. Your birthday cake collapses from the weight of the candles.

6. You go to put on the clothes you wore home from the party
   and there aren't any.

7. You turn on the news and they're displaying emergency routes
   out of your city.

8. The woman you've been seeing on the side begins to look like
   your wife.

9. Your twin sister forgets your birthday.

10. You wake up to discover that your waterbed broke and then
    you realize that you don't have a waterbed.

11. Your horn goes off accidentally and remains stuck as you
    follow a group of Hell's Angels on the motorway.

12. Your wife wakes up feeling amorous and you have a headache.


```
**************************************************************************
**************************************************************************
```

HOW TO GET ALONG
AT THE OFFICE

If it rings, put it on hold;

If it clanks, call the repairman;

If it whistles, ignore it;

If it's a friend, take a break;

If it's a boss, look busy;

If it talks, take notes;

If it's handwritten, type it;

If it's typed, copy it;

If it's copied, file it;

If it's Friday, forget it!

We the willing
led by the unknowing
are doing the impossible
for the ungrateful.
We have done so much
for so long
with so little
we are now qualified
to do anything
with nothing!

A FABLE FOR SECRETARIES

When the body was first made, all parts wanted to be Boss. The Brain said, "Since I control everything and do all the thinking, I should be Boss."

The Feet said, "Since I carry man where he wants to go, and get him in position to do what the Brain wants, I should be Boss."

The Hands said, "Since I must do all the work and earn all the money to keep the rest of you going, I should be Boss."

And so it went with the Heart, the Ears, the Lungs, etc. And finally the Arsehole spoke up and demanded to be the Boss. All the other parts laughed and laughed at the idea of an Arsehole being Boss.

The Arsehole was so angered that he blocked himself off and refused to function. Soon the Brain was feverish, the Eyes crossed and aching. The Feet were too weak to walk; the Hands hung limply at the sides; the Heart and Lungs struggled to keep going.

All pleaded with the Brain to relent and let the Arsehole be Boss. And so it happened. All the other parts did all the work, and the Arsehole just bossed and passed out a lot of shit.

THE MORAL:

YOU DON'T HAVE TO BE A BRAIN TO BE A BOSS, JUST AN ARSEHOLE

WOULD YOU BE VERY UPSET
IF I ASKED YOU TO TAKE
YOUR ASININE PROBLEM DOWN THE HALL?

A CLEAN DESK IS A SIGN OF A SICK MIND

MEDITATION

How is it, Lord,
That I who am so wise
and knowing . . .
Gifted in the ways of language
and perception . . .
So understanding . . .
Alert to every nuance and suggestion,
And deeply read as well,
Should screw up with such regularity?

Amen

SECRETARY BURNOUT

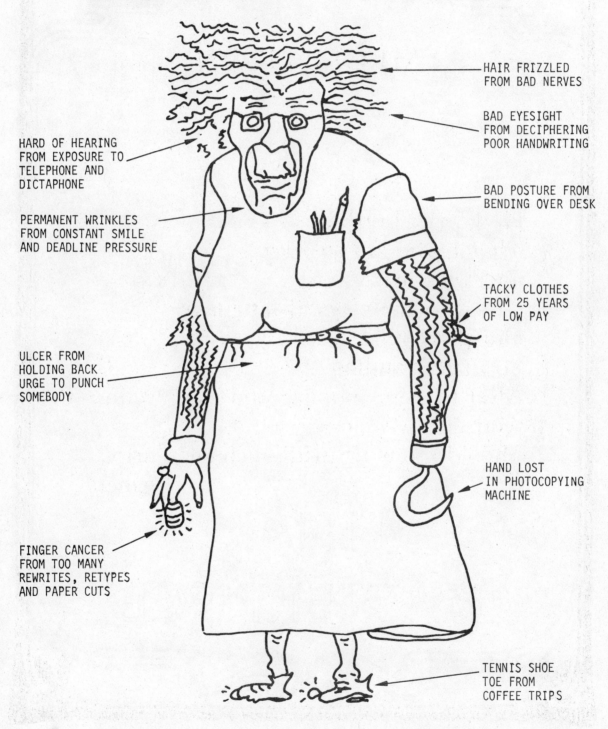

HAIR FRIZZLED
FROM BAD NERVES

BAD EYESIGHT
FROM DECIPHERING
POOR HANDWRITING

HARD OF HEARING
FROM EXPOSURE TO
TELEPHONE AND
DICTAPHONE

BAD POSTURE FROM
BENDING OVER DESK

PERMANENT WRINKLES
FROM CONSTANT SMILE
AND DEADLINE PRESSURE

TACKY CLOTHES
FROM 25 YEARS
OF LOW PAY

ULCER FROM
HOLDING BACK
URGE TO PUNCH
SOMEBODY

HAND LOST
IN PHOTOCOPYING
MACHINE

FINGER CANCER
FROM TOO MANY
REWRITES, RETYPES
AND PAPER CUTS

TENNIS SHOE
TOE FROM
COFFEE TRIPS

SURE GOD CREATED
MAN BEFORE WOMAN

BUT THEN
YOU ALWAYS MAKE
A ROUGH DRAFT
BEFORE...

THE
FINAL
MASTERPIECE

GOAHEAD, YOU SON-OF-A-BITCH,
GIVE IT A TURN!
I WORK BETTER UNDER PRESSURE!

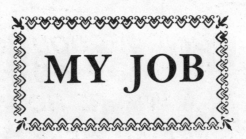

MY JOB

It's not my place to run the train
The whistle I can't blow
It's not my place to say how far
The train's allowed to go
It's not my place to shoot off steam
Nor even clang the bell
But let the damn thing
Jump the track . . .
AND SEE WHO CATCHES HELL!

BE KIND AND GOOD NATURED AND YOU'LL

ALWAYS GET YOUR REWARD!!

IF YOU ARE UNHAPPY

Once upon a time, there was a nonconforming
sparrow who decided not to fly south for the winter.
However, soon the weather turned so cold that he
reluctantly started to fly south. In a short time ice
began to form on his wings and he fell to earth in
a barnyard, almost frozen. A cow passed by and
crapped on the little sparrow. The sparrow thought
it was the end. But, the manure warmed him and
defrosted his wings. Warm and happy, able to
breathe, he started to sing. Just then a
large cat came by and hearing the chirping,
investigated the sounds.
The cat cleared away the manure, found the
chirping bird and promptly ate him.

The moral of the story:

1. Everyone who shits on you is not necessarily your enemy.
2. Everyone who gets you out of the shit is not necessarily your friend.
3. And, if you're warm and happy in a pile of shit, keep your mouth shut.

TO MY CRITICS

When I am in a sober mood—
 I worry work and think.
When I am in a drunken mood—
 I gamble fight and drink.

But when all my moods are over—
 And the worst has come to pass—
I hope they bury me upside down
 So the world can kiss my arse.

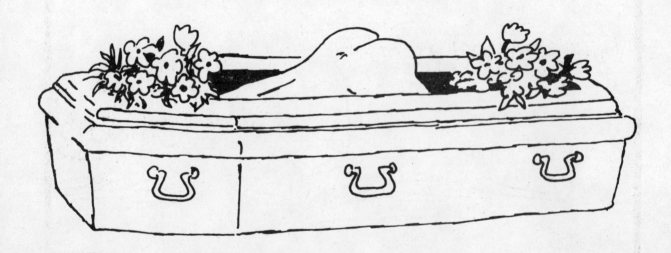